Believing God

Published by Spines Publishing Platform
ISBN: 978-965-578-457-2

For my sister, Lisa

Believing God

By Hikeem Wallace

Contents

Acknowledgments

I would like to thank my brothers, Donald and Tyrone, who have poured and then pressed into me; that change is a challenge, but it can be good. What sound advice this has been for the acumen of writing this devotional.

I would be remiss and negligent if I did not express a special thank you to: Ms. Zenitha Brown, my editor; Mr. Antwan Twizzy Campbell, my book illustrator; and my supporting cast from Molded 4 Ministry.

My heart is humbled and full of the many family members and myriad of friends who have prayed for this book to be born. May God get all the glory.

Introduction

As time moves forward and moments become fragmented, there are diversified progressions that parallel the sophistication of life and the difficulties of sustaining healing and wholeness.

You are the *"isness"* of now as a human being. It engulfs the emotions of great expectations or extreme frustration. These polar opposites are the results of what the heart and mind perceive it to be. The world will line up its allies to exalt you to the highest level; then, in a split second, it will crush you under the rubble you once stood on. My beloved sister, Lisa, wrote before her death that the providence of God is what harnesses you from the storms of life. His gigantic hands are clenched together to protect us from the *"isness"* that could have been.

"I have told you these things, so that in me you may have peace. In this world you will have

trouble. But take heart! I have overcome the world." (John 16:33 NIV)

No one is immune from the tragedy or traumas that life can hurl at us. A brush with death, escaping through the flames to see another day. A polarizing situation that has isolated you from family and friends. The throws of financial woes that can disrupt plans for a prosperous future. A rare disease that severs the strength of a relationship. There are a multitude of chaotic and climatic circumstances that can enter the front door of our life.

So, how do we prepare ourselves to embrace the inevitable and the inescapable that is to come? The philosophy of *"oughtness"* is that we must do something in order to achieve a desired end. This has its truth to a certain degree, for our decisions are worked out through the determinate purposes that have been ordained by God. Given the prognosis of the problem and the justification of it, how do we shift the dynamics so that we can maintain the concept of being victorious instead of becoming a victim? The promises of God are the living hope that covers and comforts us through every circumstance in life.

I pray that these thirty devotions will add some insight and illumination into how God from eternity past has predestined to save us to Himself.

God Has Not Forgotten You

In Genesis 21, we get a parenting tip from God, who is concerned about the rearing of children. In verses 8 through 16, we get the record of Hagar and her child being sent out from their surroundings that she embraced and felt a sense of security within. This parallels Adam and Eve, who were sent out from the Garden of Eden to embrace a new life absent from their provider, who is God. The author, Aldous Huxley, writes about the horror and the challenges of facing a brand-new future. Many of us have experienced the difficulties and dismal outcomes of walking this path alone. This woman was sent out to wean her child and to provide for their future in the absence of a male figure. How many of us have felt abandoned and the absence of a loving touch from someone who was supposed to be standing in the gap? The grime reality sets up a poverty-stricken future without hope. It is one thing to face trials and tests in the season of hopelessness; there is another thing to go through this adversity: carrying that weight on your narrow shoulders alone.

The righteous is delivered out of trouble, and the wicked cometh in his stead. (Proverbs 11:8 KJV)

Solomon is communicating that we must remember that God is our caretaker and our trust is in Him. Although this woman was sent out into the world and not given a fighting chance, her faith needed to remain strong in knowing the character of God. It is important to keep track of your history with God and how He has shown Himself strong on your behalf. This is a testimony of God's affectual love for His child that we all need to be reminded of as we travel through life's storm. If we know anything, we can attest that God's number one attribute is love. So, Solomon writes that God Himself will deliver His children from trouble and will place that trying circumstance at the doorstep of the wicked. Verse 17 says that God heard the voice of the child and told Hagar to fear not, for He was going to supply for their future.

And God heard the voice of the lad; and the angel of God called Hagar out of heaven, and

*said unto her, What aileth thee, Hagar? fear not;
for God hath heard the voice of the lad where he
is. (Genesis 21:17 KJV)*

In times of trouble, we find the faithfulness of
God to shine even brighter. He is not a God who
treats us as orphans, but He takes delight in us
while delivering us from harm. In verse 20, we
see the sustaining power of God remaining with
the child as he grew. This is the God of the
Bible, Jehovah Shammah, the God who walks
and talks with us throughout our journey. In
Genesis 17:20, we get the account of Ismael, the
child of Hagar, who was sent out into the
wilderness. God said I have heard thee. I have
blessed him. I will make him fruitful. I will
multiply him exceedingly with twelve princes. I
will make him a great nation.

The promises of God are not forgotten, and
they will come to fruition according to His
divine purposes and His plan. This was the
promise of God, past tense, before Hagar and
the child were sent out into their wilderness
experience. The greatness of God is that He
foreknew your problems before they were
present knowledge to you. The goodness of
God is that He will come alongside you to
answer your prayers and give you an expected
hope. May the Lord give you an open heart to
believe that you are never alone and that His
presence will be nigh unto you for protection so

that you will have a peace that surpasses all human understanding.

Prayer: May your faith not waiver, but remain strong in the promises of God. May the manifestation of His mercies abide with you and give you the strength to finish strong. Amen

A Benediction To The Beloved

Many of us have had moments where we needed to be affirmed and appreciated. It is the sense of being validated, knowing that we have worth. Standing alone, separated from the crowd, is no walk in the park; it is like a stroll through the desert plains. Everyone welcomes an ally who will stand with them in the heat of a battle. This may be the reason why a myriad of believers choose Psalm 27:10 as there swan song.

When my father and mother forsake me, then the LORD will take me up. (Psalm 27:10 KJV)

David writes this as a universal principle that speaks to the goodness of God, who would never hide His face from the hurting nor shut His ears to those who are crying out to Him. But

His loving-kindness is always on display. The Scriptures speak of this remarkable fact that our Father never sleeps nor slumbers. His eyes are always on us. His arms are open wide to embrace us and to give His child refreshment for the journey ahead. In Psalm 18, David describes God's care in anthropomorphic language. He says that God is my Rock, my Fortress, my Buckler, and my Shield. Each of these items is a weapon of defense that will hold off any army set in attack mode. Could we accrue this to the fact that God knows our worth more than anyone else? After all, we are created in His image and likeness, designed to give Him glory. Aristotle said, "We are works of human art." This refers to the creature discovering his reason for existence and walking into it. The Bible is full of great insights and illustrations that will galvanize the one who has the least amount of imagination or the one carrying the most doubts about having self-worth. If you read this book with great intensity and fervency, you will find Scripture after Scripture speaking of God's affinity for His beloved. The word *beloved* in Greek means one favorite. God refers to you and me as His favorite, the apple of His eye. In John 17, which some scholars have happily titled the "Priestly Prayer," Jesus prays to the Father for the Believers to be as one, just as He is with the Father. Jesus does not stop there, but petitions to the Father that the Believer would have that same oneness with Him just as He has with the

Father. How profound that we who are sinners, unlike Jesus, be called the beloved of God.

Prayer: Heavenly Father, how excellent is Your name that moves us from being the children of wrath to the sons and daughters of the Highest. Thank you for that blessed assurance that unites us into the family of God. Amen

Being Led By His Word

The Greek word for the Bible is the word *Biblos.* It has its origins in the Phoenician language, which refers to a scroll or many scrolls. We know the Bible as a large book consisting of many smaller books. It is like a bookshelf that is filled with many books of different sizes and shapes, but in this case, one book contains all the information consumed in this single volume. The beauty of these books is that the information that is communicated is not constant, but it is revelatory. Martin Luther said: "The Bible is alive, it has hands, it gets a hold of me. It has feet, it chases after me."

For the word of God is alive and active. Sharper than any double-edged sword, it penetrates even to dividing soul and spirit, joints and marrow; it

The Bible contains Scripture that will help navigate and guide us through the times of feast and times of famine. This book that God has gifted to mankind fosters the character of God, who is the author of life and the bishop of our soul. You can say that God wants us to be in the know. It is the Greek word "ginosko," which refers to having a rich understanding of the subject at hand. God used 40 authors to write the inspired Word of God under the influence of His Spirit. These men used textural language consisting of historical and revelational content that would foster a greater understanding of man's disposition apart from God. The importance of this is that we can learn valuable insights from the past and can glean into future expectancies so that our faith will not waver.

The Lord your God is with you; the mighty One will save you. He will rejoice over you. You will rest in His love; He will sing and be joyful about you. (Zephaniah 3:17 NCV)

The Bible is held by many as the epitome of integrity and truth. Year after year, this book is the number one seller across the globe, which points to the invested interest that people have for holding on to hope. God is the master builder, the One who gives life and sustains it. He is the lifter of our head, who protects and shields us from the destructive darts thrown by our adversary. His word gives us the resolve, the backbone, the fortitude to press into the difficulties of life and not give up. For example, the Apostle Paul writes to the church at Galatia to encourage them to keep going even in the time of testing.

And let us not be weary in well doing: for in due season we shall reap, if we faint not. (Galatians 6:9 KJV)

The words in this book are set forth to encourage you and give you a living hope that will not fade away. It gives you an inside look at the heart of God, who is faithful and true. His promises are spoken in simple terms, not in cryptic language; for He wants you to know *(ginosko)*. God's promises parallel His provisions for your life. He wants your days moving forward to be filled with the determination to walk with boldness and the conviction to carry out what He has decreed for your life. He has laid out the foundation and breathed in you greatness that you might walk in it.

Prayer: Lord, Your word tells us that we are to grow in the knowledge and the faith of Christ Jesus. Give us an open heart that wants to receive and abide in Your truth. May we be people that hunger and thirst after the righteousness that was found in our Savior, so that we may mirror His ways and glorify our God in Heaven. Amen

Your Gifts Are To Glorify God

The misconception of the gifts given to the Believer from the Spirit of God has plagued the Christian community since its conception back in 50 AD. Many believe the gifts were a dormant skill that was locked up in our bodies, and one day, through trial and error, its conception was introduced to the world. The Scripture tells us that when we were shaped and formed in the image of God, He did something extra to these creaturely bodies. He breathed into us His Spirit, which gives us purpose. The Greek word *gnome* refers to the mind concerning what ought to be done, a purpose that glorifies God. When God called Moses to build the Tabernacle, the plan was to involve more willing bodies to fulfill this task. We like to say the sum total of all the parts is greater than the one. In Christian circles, we would say, your gifts will make room for you. In Exodus 31, God called two men, both exceptionally skilled in their gifts, and gave them the bidding of being the artisans to craft some of the most elaborate pieces located in the sacred place in the Tabernacle. If you want to have a successful enterprise, the first step requires the appointment by God. He is the visionary and He is the orchestrator. What goes lock in step with God's call is the filling or the anointing to complete the task with excellence. Throughout the scriptures, you will read of God's vessels and their pursuit to master their craft efficiently with the assistance of the Holy Spirit. For example, when the strong man, Samson, went down to Timnath and a young lion roared as if to attack him, the scripture said that the Spirit of the LORD came mightily upon him for power and strength. Samson rent the young lion as if he was a little kid. (Judges 14:5-6 KVV) Let this sink deep down inside: there is no power in heaven or earth that is equal to God. We also must recognize that God is the rudder of the ship He navigates and guides from start to finish. Since God had placed Samson in that venue, God would be with him to give him the victory. In the first seven verses of chapter 31 of Exodus, we find the personal pronoun "I" referring to God. *I have called. I have filled. I have given. I have put wisdom. I have commanded.* This speaks to God's sovereign nature. By His power, we have divine enablement to do what we could never do in our strength. What God is showing us is that His plans for you and I are vast and it takes more than ourselves to bring it to fruition. Jesus said in *John 5:17* that the Father is working and that the Son of God is still working. God has not sat down to rest and is constantly working on perfecting you into the image of His Son. It is His Son, in whom He is well pleased (Matthew 3:17). Our attitude toward kingdom work should be diligent and a determined work that glorifies Him. Caleb, at the age of 85, still had the fire and the vigor to be victorious in what the Lord called him to. (Joshua 14:6-13) Take the testimony of Anna, who worked diligently in the house of God for 84 years after the death of her husband. There are countless stories of men and women in the Bible who stayed the course and continued to walk with God despite disappointments and discouragement in their lives. Knowing that you were created for God's glory and your gifts are for the edification of the saints, will be a powerful tool to keep you moving forward.

Prayer: Lord, we come to You in this season with our gifts of sacrifice. May they be used for the building of your kingdom and the edification of the saints. Let it bear much fruit and strengthen the faith of the fervent believer everywhere. Amen

Your Steps Are Ordered
For Success

As you rise in the morning, do you take notice of the activity of your limbs and ligaments? It is clear to see that they are functioning according to their designed purpose. Does this give you pause to ingratiate God, the giver of every good and perfect gift? Maybe you had thought through a plan, but the resources were not there to finalize the process, and miraculously, an unexpected partner stepped in to seal the deal. If we trace the pathway that led to our satisfaction, we will see that our steps were ordered by the Lord. Every step along the way, the imprint of God's hand divinely ordered your outcome for good success. God's ways are not set as an opposition to hinder, but as a helpmate to give you success and to sustain it. His laws and precepts are eternal, not a temporal fix. We are given the charge to meditate on His word to be our light and to shine on our pathway, navigating us to greater successes to come.

Keep this Book of the Law always on your lips, meditate on it day and night, so that you may be careful to do everything written in it. Then you will be prosperous and successful. (Joshua 1:8 NIV)

This verse is pregnant with power and the persistence to press into what God has called you to accomplish. The history of this verse is centered around God's people following the Prophet Moses out of Egypt, a place where they were enslaved. Moses dies, and now, God has placed the mantle of moving the people forward on the leadership of Joshua. When change enters our lives, we have the tendency to resist and wait for the final results before we believe. Change causes agitation and a disturbance in our peace, for it knocks down the walls that insulate our security. The feeling of not being safe creates doubt and shifts our minds to seeing only failure. But God, who is the author of new beginnings, has a plan for your success that was predetermined and was worked out in eternity past.

The God of the Bible is not defined by time or space and cannot be defeated by the hands of man's manipulation. God is omnipotent. He has all the power to manifest anything by His sovereign will. God is omniscient, for He has knowledge of all things from its conception to the death of it. He is immutable, for His character cannot be swayed by the craftiness of evil. God's omnipresence is what gives us the assurance that our gifts are ordered for success. When God is walking with you, His power fortifies your accomplishments. The Greek word *"exousia"* refers to God's power and authority to sway the outcome in your favor. Every plan that He puts in place fulfills what He proposed it to accomplish. Just like many of us, the people of Joshua's day did not trust in the sovereignty of God and His faithfulness to keep His word, until they saw the fruit that it reaped.

God gives charge to Joshua to move forward without hesitancy. He commissions Joshua with the same power as the first leader, Moses. Affirming in him the confidence needed for success to lead His people into the land of promise. God said to Joshua three times, the superlative term for the highest degree, "Be strong and very courageous." A firm, straightforward message that we need to sow in our spirit as we walk into the divine purpose that we were created for. The words of God are trustworthy and true: be strong and very courageous; the LORD God is with thee. What a strong affirmation to know that God is walking with you for a bright future and for good success.

Prayer: Our praises and glory to our Great and Wise King, the One who has ordered our steps and has taken delight in our ways. You have removed the stumbling blocks and the obstacles that have stood in the way of our success. May we continue to walk in that light that shines forth to the fertile grounds and fields of great harvest. Amen

The Marks Of A Great Leader

Now it came to pass in the third year of Hoshea son of Elah king of Israel, that Hezekiah the son of Ahaz king of Judah began to reign. (2Kings 18:1 KJV)

Hoshea was the last reigning of 19 kings of the northern kingdom of Israel. This role of leadership came to a screeching halt, when the Assyrian army came and dismantled the northern kingdom, exiling the people throughout the world in the year 722 BC. Meanwhile, in the southern kingdom of Judah, the people were inaugurating a new king to lead them. The old leadership under Ahaz was wicked and had a disregard for the reverence of the LORD. The people who were called by God's name did not serve nor sacrifice to Him. Instead, they recognized and gave reverence to the foreign gods of their neighboring nations. Hezekiah stepped into the leading role at the age of twenty-five and led with more maturity than his father, Ahaz. It was very clear from the beginning that the great King, the Lord of Glory, who dresses us up for success, had His hands on Hezekiah. Just a footnote, more pages in the scripture are given to Hezekiah than any other king of the northern or the southern reign of Israel. His impact was critical for the survival of the southern kingdom when it was faced with adversity from opposing world powers such as Assyria and Babylon.

So, we must ask ourselves, what did Hezekiah do that made his leadership different from the other kings? The first thing that Hezekiah did was to have a campaign for reform. Unlike the other kings, Hezekiah was sold out for the LORD. He dismantled every place of worship that honored the false gods of the world. This included the high places, the altars and even the bronze serpent that was worshiped since the campaign of Moses. (Numbers 21:8-9) Hezekiah's administration was ruled with righteousness, which reflected a different tone toward the things of God. So, in the fourteenth year of his reign, the Assyrian army threatened to attack Judah. Hezekiah prayed to the LORD and interceded for his people.

Then Isaiah the son of Amos sent a message to Hezekiah: "This is what the LORD, the God of Israel, says: I have heard your prayer concerning Sennachrib king of Assyria. (2 Kings 19:20 NIV)

You cannot put into words the gravity of the weight that is lifted off your shoulders when you hear that God has heard your prayers. It exudes confidence and gives conviction that you are in good hands. It all starts with having that intimate relationship with the Lord. He alone is the only One that has the power and the wherewithal to deliver from the fiery furnace that will cancel your future. Because Hezekiah used his leadership platform to honor God, the LORD honored him with a covering for the people and the comfort of being free from the shackles of bondage. May the Lord give you godly leadership that will exude and examine the explicit message of trusting in the Lord for everything in spite of what it looks like.

Prayer: I thank You, Lord, for Your great wisdom in helping us become leaders that can carry the mantle of Your Spirit. I ask that You sow into us the courage of Hezekiah and give us the skills to be the commander of our ship. Let us carry the vision that You have decreed for us to follow, so that victory will always be ours. Amen

Being In Position To Be Used

The etymology of the word "position" comes from the Latin to mean to put or to place. The idea is to get that person, place, or thing in its correct spot. Growing up in a city known for basketball icons, we used the term cherry picking. It referred to a player who made a deliberate effort to not run the full length of the court on his defensive possession, but decided to remain on the offensive side, waiting for a pass for an uncontested layup. Short of cheating, it was an offensive strategy used to help score points. In order for this scenario to work, this player had to be in a position to receive the pass to score the bucket. Likewise, a man used by God must be spiritually attuned to hear His voice, so that he will have clear instructions to do the Lord's bidding.

Now, we must remember that anywhere God places us, it has an ultimate purpose. His plans are always for good and the redeeming work in bringing man back to his rightful place. The Lord always has a remnant to do His bidding and sometimes it is the cherry picker who waits patiently for the ball to be thrown his way. From an ontological view, it would appear that the Lord just randomly chooses people and sends them out unprepared to be devoured by the world. God never sends us out to do a divine work that we are not first spiritually inclined to do.

In Jeremiah 38, there was a man by the name of Ebedmelech, an Ethiopian eunuch, who worked in the king's house. Ebedmelech was called by God to preserve the life of one of God's anointed. Ebedmelech carried the mantle of courage and he possessed the heart of compassion, which gave him the fortitude and the faith to accomplish this assignment. The Scripture said that after he heard the message of Jeremiah being in danger, he went immediately to the king. (Jeremiah 38:7-8) What is implied is that Ebedmelech gave no thought to how this would inconvenience his plans for that day. But his focus was solely on saving a human being's life.

A constant theme that is woven throughout God's word is that He looks at the heart of a man, not his disposition in the community. God uses ordinary people to do extraordinary work. Ebedmelech had no right to approach the king, coming from a cosmological view where monarchs did not entertain the company of a servant. A eunuch was a man who was castrated to guard or to be a servant for a harem of women or those in the king's quarters. Ebedmelech's place was not to be in the presence of the king to make inquiries, but to make his presence felt amongst the women for their protection. On a certain day, Ebedmelech just happened to be in position according to God's providence and heard a conversation on how they were going to destroy Jeremiah. The Ethiopian eunuch went to the king and demanded that he do something to save the man of God. What boldness and the brass that this man carried to go to the top official in the country and insist that he take action. Being in the presence of God will give you the fortitude and the faith to do something that you would not ordinarily do. Having faith in your tool belt will give you the spiritual muscle to push fear aside and proceed with the call on your life.

And He said unto them, Why are ye so fearful? how is it that ye have no faith? (Mark 4:40 KJV)

When you exercise the faith of a mustard seed, high-ranking officials will listen and grant your request. King Zedekiah gave Ebedmelech thirty men and the resources to save the life of Jeremiah. May the testimony of Ebedmelech be a light to your soul that will ignite your faith, so that the Lord will put you in a position to be used in this season.

Prayer: Lord God, our Jehovah Nessi, I ask that You strategically position us as pawns to be used for Your glory. May our allegiance be to You and the strengthening of our faith. Give us the attributes of patience and persistence so that we will be poised to move forward in Your appointed time. Amen

Exhorting The Gift Of Encouragement

The fabric of life is so fragile: one minute, your heart is filled with delight and much gratification; moments later, you feel the heaviness of despair and death to your dreams. Your emotions are walking a tightrope that is dangling over the choice to run on or to end it all. This was the life of David, the anointed king of Israel. In spite of David's many victories over his adversaries, he was fighting a losing battle within. The root cause was his precarious decisions concerning his family. The dangers of putting stock in the affairs of the world and leaving your home depleted of time and resources will haunt you in your future endeavors.

In 1 Samuel 30:1-6, we have a portrait of David's wilderness season. He was on the run from Saul, the present king of Israel and was forced to hide out in caves and abandoned fields. David attached himself to a group of outcasts who were living without hope and found himself thrust into the leadership role to bring reform. David led these men to win many battles against their adversaries and, with each victory, their disposition changed from being discouraged to being encouraged about their present life. After the battle at Ziklag, the city name means pressed down, David and his men found their town burned to the ground. What made this scene more depressing was that their wives, their sons and their daughters were taken captive. David, as the leader of this group, found himself shouldering the blame for the loss of everything that these men had started to regain. Let us keep in mind that David was not isolated from this great loss; he had family and financial ties that were taken away. A good leader displays the characteristic of compassion when a tragic moment touches someone dear to you. Your heart breaks for each person who has suffered devastation. So, the added weight of David's loss compounded with each man's loss is enough to lead them into a season of doubt and disbelief. As the leader, all eyes are fixed on you to bring back a revival of hope and to restore confidence where it has faded. The first thing that David did was to go into prayer to the God who always has His eyes on us. This is encouraging because God does not need us to fill in the blanks for our desired end. God did not create you and me to dwell in the shadow of doom and gloom nor live a life of doubt or constant defeat. God wants us to thrive and to be triumphant, pointing to Him for the many battles that He has won. This is what David needed to be deposited in his spirit. This battle was not his, but the LORDS. When we come to that cross-road when the cares of life begin to wear on us, we too must remember that God is our burden bearer; a mighty fortress is our God.

So, David, God's next anointed king, had to stand tall and walk with fervor, knowing that the LORD was on his side to help him win the battle within. Sometimes, you need to speak of victory while you are in the midst of your test.

And David was greatly distressed; for the people spake of stoning him, because the soul of all the people was grieved, every man for his sons and his daughters: but David encouraged himself in the LORD his God. (1 Samuel 30:6 KJV)

The Greek word *parakaleo* refers to giving comfort while urging the importance of keeping going. David's faith was in the LORD's ability to win the day. We, too, must lay aside our pride to get the job done and place it in God's word, which instills confidence and conviction in our spirit. One way of being encouraged is to rehearse and regurgitate what God has spoken over you. His promises will come to pass, for

He is well and able to finish that great work that He has started in you. David internalized that the weight was too much for him to bear and that his soul needed rest.

Come to Me, all you who are weary and burdened, and I will give you rest. (Matthew 11:28 NIV)

Jesus makes the plea that when life gets difficult and danger keeps heading your way, come to Him and lay those troubles at His feet. So, David went to the One that he had a working relationship with, Jehovah El Shaddai, the Almighty God. David also knew that the God he worshiped was always available and easily accessible. The arms of God are always open, ready to receive and to redeem you from the clutches of destruction. I asked a question earlier: what do you do when you feel the weight of the world on your shoulders? You encourage yourself in the Lord. You go to God in prayer, expressing your concerns and your petitions. You recite the word of God and how He promises to fight for you. You begin to worship God by thanking Him for what He is about to do. You stand firm and watch God show Himself strong on your behalf.

Prayer: Lord, our ears are pinned back to hear Your word that will navigate and guide us. Let

our hearts be open to receive those marching orders that will position us to serve in Your house. Give us a servant's heart so that we may be a voice of encouragement to everyone who enters our space. The Bible says that kind words are like honey: sweet to the soul and good for the body. Amen

Your Prayers Can Transform Change

Imagine having a relationship with a good friend who had your heart and you would sacrifice everything to see the blessings of God come their way. But their view of life differed from yours. Their ethics of good and evil did not parallel the teachings that you were brought up on. This person did not have an open mind about change and possessed an unwillingness to embrace the social pyrolysis of giving to those in need. If you brought up a valid point, they would dismiss it, for they were the final authority. They had a controlling mindset, which provoked change according to the dogmatic thoughts that were entertained in their mind. The words that continually came from their mouth paralleled the lofty thoughts of Rome: "The world begins here and ends here." Now imagine this is God having an intimate relationship with you and me.

Hezekiah rested with his ancestors. And Manasseh his son succeeded him as king. (2 Kings 20:21 NIV)

The Scripture tells us that Hezekiah was one of the last righteous kings of Judah, and now his son Manasseh takes his stead. Manasseh became king at the age of 12 and reigned for fifty-two years, longer than any other king in Judah. His tenure as king was considered the most decadent and degenerated time for God's people.

Moreover, Manasseh shed blood very much, till he had filled Jerusalem from one end to another; beside his sin wherein he made Judah to sin, in doing that which was evil in the sight of the LORD. (2 Kings 20:16 KJV)

This comes on the heel of God protecting Judah from the attacks from its most powerful adversaries from the north. Manasseh manifested a total transformation in the kingdom of Judah from the previous administration under his father's leadership. How can a child grow up in the same household of god-fearing parents and surrounded by great, influential minds embrace a philosophy that is apathetic and callous? Many of us have pondered that same thought when looking at some of our friends who had the same advantages. It puzzles us to no end, for we are told that the apple does not roam too far from the tree. However, prayer brings clarity and concise answers when human wisdom fails. The prayers of Hezekiah and Hephzibah, the mother of Manasseh, were instrumental in bringing him back into the arms of God. One of the parenting tips from the Lord that bodes well with raising children is interceding on their behalf to God and teaching them His precepts. Using these two building blocks as a foundation for their future, will manifest a good return.

Train up a child in the way he should go: and when he is old, he will not depart from it. (Proverbs 22:6 KJV)

As we grow older, we should also become wiser, for the maturation in how we think should parallel the years that we have spent walking on earth. We should take a daily inventory to examine where we are in fulfilling our divine purpose. The training is the development of a mindset that exudes the gifts and the perfecting of it. God was clear when He shaped and molded you into His crowning jewel adorned for good works. It all starts with developing the prayer life that beckons God's attention, whereby we can petition to the Almighty and patiently wait for Him to answer. Prayer is the unique experience of having the ear of the Sovereign Lord.

Near the end of Manasseh's reign as king of Judah, he was exiled by the king of Assyria and afflicted by his enemies. Manasseh humbled himself and returned to the LORD. (2 Chronicles 33:12-13 KJV) His prayer of repentance is a bountiful work that deserves a separate devotion. It can be found in the Septuagint Bible.

Prayer: Heavenly Father, I come with a thankful heart that You have the power to redeem and regenerate the most hardened heart and transform it into one of flesh. Let us never forget that every man or woman can change and be used for Your glory. You are the Potter, and we are the clay that can be shaped and molded into the image of Your Beloved Son. Amen

A Different Approach

The beauty of God is His desire to forgive so that we, as Believers, can continue to move forward. He removes the robe of heaviness from our sinful acts and clothes us with His compassion. God is not like man. God chooses grace as a different approach.

But the people there did not welcome Him, because He was heading for Jerusalem. When the disciples James and John saw this, they asked, "Lord, do you want us to call fire down from heaven to destroy them?" But Jesus turned and rebuked them. (Luke 9:53-55 NIV)

The time was set by the Father for Jesus to go to the cross, the ultimate act of sacrificing His life to redeem the lost souls of men. Jesus and His disciples were heading to Jerusalem, the appointed place for His suffering. On the way, some men from a Samaritan village denied them passage to go through. This was critical, because this was the quickest route that led to Jerusalem. The first lesson we learn in geometry is that the quickest way between two points is a straight line. The scripture teaches us that God operates on an appointed time, although He is not defined nor dependent on time. But Jesus fixed His face like a flint and continued to press forward to His passion. This is a lesson that we all need to embrace. Your assignment from the Father should be taken so seriously that we give no room for anything to hinder our progress to accomplish it. Whenever you set your heart to master something great, know that the adversary is on the prowl to prohibit you from crossing that finish line of completion. Jesus was pressing forward to Jerusalem and it was His disciples who gave Him the greatest consternation, for they suggested something that is the polar opposite of compassion. We must be careful not to buy into the outside voices that operate contrary to our destiny. Here, Jesus is showing the world the greatest sacrifice known to man, dying for His brother.

For even the Son of man came not to be ministered unto, but to minister, and to give His life a ransom for many. (Mark 10:45 KJV)

Although Jesus was given inhospitable treatment by the Samaritan men, He knew that His purpose was greater than the adversity that was before Him.

Let's rewind Jesus and His disciples are walking down the road, and out of nowhere, a group of men jump from behind the bushes to form a wall so that no one could get past. The Scripture tells us that two of Jesus's close disciples, James and John, wanted to call down fire from heaven to destroy these men. Jesus takes this opportunity to give His disciples a teachable moment that reflects the grace and the mercy of the Father.

The scriptures are replete with many teachable moments for us to glean and to grow stronger in the ways of God. In this moment, Jesus wanted the disciples and future Believers to know His mission given to Him from the Father. In Hebrew, the word mission signifies being sent from one place to another place for a purpose. Jesus pressing into His purpose was the greater good, for He was moving forward to save lives, not sending down fire to destroy life. We are going to face some difficulties as we travel the road to fulfill our destiny, but we must look forward to the glory of finishing our course. Often, in the heat of battle, we want the worst for our enemies, for they are a stumbling block to our aspirations and dreams. But I come to tell you that your divisive actions are the greater hindrance to achieving what God has for you.

When your mind is focused on the problem, less potential energy is being used to move forward. I have found that the more I examine the life of Jesus and walk in His ways, the fewer foes and failures I have faced.

Prayer: Heavenly Father, You have created this universe and everything in it. You have masterfully placed everything in its divine order. You orchestrated the movement of the sun and the moon, so that man has light and the comfort to dwell in it. Let us be mindful that You are in control, and nothing happens unless it first passes Your holy desk. You have given us the decree that vengeance is Yours and not ours, that You have the power to make righteousness abound, and the keys to every man's heart. So, Lord, we place our hurt and our pain in Your hands so that You may bring healing and wholeness to our situation. Amen

No One Knows Your Worth Like God

The Bible teaches us that you are in God's intellect, which means that He intimately knows you and can discern your actions by what you think and will do. This all took place before you were conceived in your mother's womb. God had a purpose, a set plan for you to prosper and to walk in greatness. You were born in the fullness of time to redeem the blessing that would chart your course and fulfill that divine purpose. If God revealed to us the intricacies of His plan, it would scare most of us to death. But this is not God's work one reason why God shares with us small bite sizes before the plan is augmented and fleshed out. The vastness of the mind of God is too much for our finite minds to comprehend, so He nourishes us with His word to build us up in the maturation and the illumination of who we are in Him. Outside of the will of God, we are instruments of a useless passion. In Him, we have the ability to move the mountain of doubt. When I hear the word doubt, I can hear the church say: Is there anything too hard for God?

Behold, I am the LORD, the God of all flesh: is there anything too hard for Me? (Jeremiah 32:27 KJV)

We are speaking about Jehovah El Shaddai, the Almighty God who laid the foundation of this world and fashioned every created thing to walk upon it. He commanded the light to rise in the morning and for it to go down in the evening. He has the power to create something out of nothing and to bring life out of death. This is the God who shaped and molded you into a living creature with purpose. The Scripture says that God calls us His crowning jewel, the apple of His eye, whom He protects.

For this is what the Lord Almighty says: "After the Glorious One has sent me against the nations that have plundered you for whoever touches you touches the apple of His eye. (Zechariah 3:8 NIV)

He uses His word of truth to encourage you and to give you strength for life's journey. God knows your worth and desires to have an intimate relationship with you. The macroeconomics of the 21st century deals with putting a numerical value on everything that is tangible; this way, it can be easily divided into classifications. The Scripture tells us that Jesus was turned over to his enemies for thirty pieces of silver. Biblical scholars believed that thirty pieces of silver were worth four months of earnings in the first century. Today, a human being is worth 10 million dollars, according to economists. This sounds like an incredible amount of money, but in the eyes of the Maker of heaven and earth, the price is too low. I am sure that it breaks God's heart to see many of us living beneath our worth. Fear is a direct correlation to why we keep coming up short. The word of God tells us to go and venture out, but we reject it and live our days close to the vest.

The LORD mocks fear and does not turn His back from the sword of danger. This is the God who created you in His image and His likeness (Genesis 1:26 KJV). Just as God spoke these things into existence through His divine imperative, He speaks life into what He decreed for you to accomplish. It is not a strange phenomenon for those who are closest to you to not understand or easily buy into your walk. In Mark 6:1-6, there is a narrative that speaks of Jesus feeling the same condemnation that many of us have felt when it comes to not being recognized as God's chosen vessel. In the Jewish tradition of that day, it was expected for a son to follow in the footsteps of his father. So, when Jesus stepped into the synagogue to teach on the Sabbath day, His family and friends were offended. They purposed in their spirit that Jesus was the son of a carpenter. Therefore, His vocation in life was to be just a carpenter. The Greek word for carpenter is *tekton,* a craftsman in the area of woodwork. Those close to you, much like the family and friends of Jesus, will often find it hard to fathom your worth in the Father's eyes. But God does not look at the external things that surround us, He sets His gaze at our hearts and sees our potential. Moving forward, may you begin to take steps that will allow the word of God to be nourished in your spirit as you shut out the voices of discouragement.

And He marveled because of their unbelief. And He went round about the villages teaching. (Mark 6:6 KJV)

Christ knew what the Father had spoken in His ear and He knew that God's plan always comes to fruition. God has equipped you and empowered you from the start and will see you finish your course.

Prayer: Lord, I ask that You will search our hearts and take out anything that will hinder us from doing the bidding that You have spoken over our lives. Replace it with the fruit of the Spirit that harnesses every gift under Your divine control. Amen

The Lord Provides And Protects

This is an easy sell; if we could rewind the clock to the moment of conception to the caring of our present needs, the hand of God has always been present. Psalm 18, which speaks directly to the nurturing attribute of God, gives us an inside look behind the curtain of His care and His sustainability for us. The Psalm opens with praise for God, who has heard our prayers and our petitions. The psalmist, who many believe is King David, speaks of God as our rock, our fortress, and our deliverer; the One who is our high tower where we can run to for protection. Moses earlier used these words, and now David speaks of these words as a metaphor for God's strength. Strength giving us the fortitude to move forward when we are weak and frail. Moses said to the people of that day it was by the hand of God's strength that we broke free from the bondage of Egyptian rule.

(Exodus 13:14 KJV) Many of us have had situations that tied our hands and took away our vision for a brighter future. The God that both Moses and David speak of is the same God that abides with us in times of trouble. The pictorial image of a fortress is a large castle with sustainable walls that becomes our place for defense. The mind of David is thinking of God protecting us from a large-scale attack or an onslaught from our enemies. There is a similar term the Bible speaks of that parallels this idea: it is the word high tower. This was a place that you could run to and hide, giving you comfort and the confidence that your enemies could not reach you. What made this place so unique was its high walls, which made it almost impossible for any man to scale. When God sends His protection, it is like the walls of the high tower: no man has the power to infiltrate the promises that He has spoken over your situation. We have become survivors because of the Savior's redeeming work that has destroyed the yoke that the adversary has tried to place around our necks. For all intentional purposes, the battle that you are entertaining is not your war; it is God's. I know that this does not make logical sense, but it is good theological sense. A good father will do anything to protect his children. Moreover, God is the greatest Father, He will move heaven and earth to protect you. Many of us have escaped dangerous episodes that have come close to destroying us, but the Lord has been there to hide us under His wings of protection.

Have mercy on me, my God, have mercy on me, for in You I take refuge. I will take refuge in the shadows of Your wings until the disaster has passed. (Psalm 57:1 NIV)

David also wrote about God's deliverance. This is something that we all can attest to, that God is a deliverer not only from our present enemies, but our future adversaries as well. The fact that God knows our ending from our beginning, sheds light on His providence to safeguard us in walking into enemy territory. The Greek word *aphesis* means to be set free or rescued from something that is marked dangerous to our existence. Whenever God comes to rescue us, His purpose in deliverance is always partnered with moving us to a higher level of righteousness.

He rules the world in righteousness and judges the people with equity. (Psalm 9:8 NIV)

The word righteousness is the quality of being "Just" or showing fairness. So, when God delivers us, there are teachable moments that we can learn, which will help us to display fairness and to show virtue. When someone comes to help you and gives you aided assistance, virtue is one attribute of displaying a sense of gratitude. It is the conformity to conduct ourselves in a moral and righteous way. As Believers, we give God the praise and the glory for His lovingkindness. God also has been our horn of salvation. He has reclaimed and redeemed the things that we have lost. The most important thing that we need is that relationship with the Father and His Son. A good father is always concerned with the well-being of his child and his heart is consistently looking for opportunities to provide and to protect his own. Each morning that we open our eyes and experience the blessing of a new day is a reflection of God's goodness and His mercies to preserve us.

Prayer: Heavenly Father, we come with a humble heart to magnify and exalt Your name, for there is no other God who has come to save and secure the life that we enjoy. May we never take for granted Your loving-kindness and the grace that is shed abroad for Your children. May we take heed of the sacrifices that Your Son made so that we can enjoy the fruit of this land. Let us never lose sight of this great salvation and the security we have in You. Amen

Recognizing The Voice
Of God

One of the puzzling things in Scripture is how the biblical writers, at times, left out the humanistic approach in how they deal with traumatic situations. For example, in Leviticus 10:1-3, we are told the story of how Aaron, the high priest's two sons, were killed. Nadab and Abihu were serving the Lord in the capacity of priests of Israel, and on a certain day, they decided to light a peculiar fire as an offering to God. What God desired for Aaron's two sons was to put a fire on the altar and arrange the wood on the fire. (Leviticus 1:7) What they did was clearly a departure from what God prescribed as a sweet, savory aroma that would be pleasing to His nostrils. Because Aaron's sons were disobedient to the commands of God and moved forward in committing what was forbidden, they were killed. It is of the utmost importance to hear the voice of God and acquiesce to perform it.

Moses, the brother of Aaron, was instructed by God to explain to him the reason for His course of action. The Scriptures tell us after Moses talked with Aaron, he remained silent.

If we had the liberty to peek into the heart of Aaron, I believe we would discover a father who was broken and angry at God. Aaron served in the capacity of leadership and was diligent in his ministry, manifesting the will of God and was called to move on as if nothing happened. But this is the precise thing that God did when His beloved Son was crucified on the cross. God moved on and continued to love us, even when it was our actions to disobey the voice of God that nailed Christ Jesus to the cross.

This story points out that there is a clarion call for Believers to hear and to obey the voice of God. The question that many of us face is how to discern God's voice from the various outside voices. This was a struggle for the Apostle Peter earlier in his walk with Christ. In Mark 8:27-33, we get the account of Peter's great confession of Jesus as the Christ and his rebuke of Jesus's going to His suffering. In this short span, we read of Peter being led by the Spirit of God and later echoing the denials of Satan.

And He spake that openly. And Peter took Him, and began to rebuke Him. But when He had turned about and looked on His disciples, He rebuked Peter, saying, Get thee behind Me, Satan: for thou savourest not the things that be of God, but the things that be of men. (Mark 8:32-33 KJV)

In that moment of time, Peter went from being the goat of the disciples to being rebuked by Jesus. Again, the scriptures breathe into us wisdom: the race is not given to the swift, but the one that endures. This means that Believers must have a steady diet of reading God's word, then listening to His voice for instructions. The Apostle Paul tells us by studying, we are taking steps that please God and that it will help us rightly divide the word of truth (2 Timothy 2:15 KJV). Peter fell short when he spoke of spiritual matters, but his understanding was coming from a world-centered view. He wanted Jesus to escape death and dwell amongst the disciples for the rest of eternity, but this was not what the voice of God was conveying to His Christ. The will of God for your life may be a path that is full of great expectations with extraordinary outcomes, or it may be one that consists of tests and trials before you receive the crown of glory. But whatever course God has charted for your life, it is of the utmost importance to hear His voice and proceed in faith.

Prayer: May the Lord direct your steps in an orderly account and anoint your path so that it will bring glory and honor to His name. Amen

Go To God For Everything In Prayer

The misnomer that many of us mistakenly think is that God is only interested in the heavy lifting in our lives. But I am from the school of thought that every concern I struggle with, I take it to the Lord in prayer. The Bible tells us that God never sleeps nor slumbers and that His eye is on those who revere Him. David wrote in Psalm 18 that God Himself comes down to rescue us in time of trouble and delivers us from the evil man. There are moments when our mind reflects on the rationale of adding another burden to the plate of God, but our mind would rest easier if we would remember that God is not like man, who has limitations.

From the end of the earth will I cry unto Thee, when my heart is overwhelmed: lead me to the rock that is higher than I. (Psalm 61:2 KJV)

In this Psalm, King David is in search of help and guidance from someone who is higher than himself. He is looking for the rock, which is the LORD. The rock is a metaphor of God being our strength and stabilizing our problematic situation. The fact of the matter is that in our human nature, when trouble comes, we organically call out to God, even if we do not have the inclination to honor Him as such. The one attribute that firm Believers and casual Believers know about God is that He is trustworthy and faithful. Proverbs 25:19 says: confidence in an unfaithful man in times of trouble is like a broken tooth and a foot out of joint. This may be a major reason why the name of God is evoked in the atmosphere at an alarming rate. David trusted in the rock, for it was his shelter from the storms of life.

In Isaiah 7:10-13, there is a spiritual lesson that should speak to our heart concerning our weariness to God. At this moment in Judah's history, they were being threatened by the Syrians, the greatest power of that day. God sent the Prophet Isaiah twice to the king of Judah to give him assurance that his people would be protected. Isaiah said to Ahaz, king of Judah, ask for a sign that will authenticate God's promise to you for protection. Just a footnote, the Jews believed that miracles were a methodology for proof, while the Gentiles looked for knowledge as the means that God had His hand in their affairs. King Ahaz responded like many of us, not wanting to wear the LORD with his trouble, but choosing to rely on his flesh to work things out.

But Ahaz said, I will not ask, neither will I tempt the LORD. (Isaiah 7:12 KJV)

If we are honest and look back at the mess that we made of our situation, many of us would pray for the opportunity to redo the steps that caused us so much regret. In Ahaz's case, it was on a collision course from doom to disaster because rejecting God's help left him with a void of experiencing the victory that the LORD had in store for him. This applies to everyone, when we sit in the place of God and dismiss His help, we are only amassing a temporary fix. When God is in it, it is a done deal. His *exousia* raises up kingdoms and tears down kingdoms; His power removes our problems and sustains us from walking back into them. Ahaz shrugged off God's help, but turned to the king of Egypt to be his covering (Isaiah 30:1-11). How many times have we decided in our mind that our course of action is to find assistance from anyone but God? How could this be knowing everything we know about Him? This is a question I believe will be answered when we get to heaven.

Praise God for His attributes of patience, being slow to anger and granting us grace. What should amaze us is the immutable character of God that does not change even when the disobedient are at the door of receiving His blessings. God, through the Prophet Isaiah, gave a sign that the LORD would step in and give safety to the people of Judah. How comforting to know that God is the same yesterday and for our tomorrow; what He has done for the people of Judah, He will surely do for you.

Therefore, the LORD Himself shall give you a sign; Behold, a virgin shall conceive, and bear a son, and shall call His name Immanuel. (Isaiah 7:14 KJV)

Prayer: Lord, I come to You rejoicing that You have made it known that You are interceding for everyone who calls on Your great name. You are our Great High Priest, who petitions the Father on our behalf and brings us thoughtless before His presence. The psalmist said: my voice will be heard in the morning; therefore, I will direct my prayer and look up. So, Lord, my heart looks for the day that our prayers will be used to unite this world in oneness that is found in You and the Father. Amen

The Danger Of False Impressions

Although you may be walking in the right direction, you may be heading the wrong way. Although your motives may be in the right place, your actions manifest a different result. What an oxymoron! This may be a reflection of how we gather information and then later process that same information. We often use the words heart and mind as if they are interchange-able, but they have distinct differences. The heart is the seat of our emotions, which is the starting point for a thought before moving in its progression of being manifested. The mind processes the thought of its validity before it is germinated into an action. So, they work off one another to produce one work. It is like a check and balance system: if one lacks its function, the other shoulders the duty to ensure its authentic-ity. For example, we say just because it is right by the letter of the law does not mean that it will sit well with everyone. The heart may want to move forward in the process because of sentimental reasons, while the mind is hard at work thinking of the dangerous and disastrous outcomes.

There is a narrative in the bible that speaks of a father who had two sons. He told the older son to do a certain work, and the son replied that he would do it. But after some time had passed, the older son decided not to do it. Likewise, the father told the younger son to do a certain work, and he said that he would not do it. But after some time had passed, the younger son regretted what he had said and did what the father had asked. The question is posed to the reader who did the right thing. I am sure that the father was pleased with the words of the older son and must have said to himself, "what a wonderful son that I have." In life, good feelings have a short shelf life. There are going to be times when those who are closest to you will let you down. It might not be intentional, but the truth of the matter is that no one can be everything to you. The painful words of rejection from the younger son must have lingered in the spirit of the father to no end. But the time of rejoicing when his disposition had changed was embraced with gladness. The older son gave a false impression that inflicted a deeper pain than the initial response of the younger son, who was more obedient to the father.

In Mark 11:12-17, we have a story of Jesus and His disciples who were leaving the town of Bethany heading to Jerusalem for the Passover celebration. This was about a 2-mile walk. Those of us who walk to build up our cardio know that you can get thirsty and crave for a meal after your journey. Well, on the route, Jesus saw a fig tree, giving the impression of having figs, although it was not its season. As Jesus approached the tree, He saw that the tree was full of leaves but barren of fruit. So, He cursed the tree and commanded that nothing would grow on it again. What makes us scratch our heads is that this tree was not due to have fruit on its branches until harvest, but Jesus, who is omniscient in knowing all things, still curses it.

This is an object lesson taught by Jesus about the dangers of false perception. Many of us have experienced the hurt and the pain of being deceived and then dragged along the road of misconception. Hearing stories of false persuasion that we took as genuine truth that turned out to give us an erroneous ending. As Jesus and His disciples continued with their journey to Jerusalem to attend the Passover, Jesus observed that the people were engaged in buying and selling. This was a feast that was held once a year to commemorate the mighty work of God delivering Israel from the strong hand of pharaoh and the Egyptian army. It was supposed to be a time of worshiping and giving adoration to the

Almighty God, but it turned out to be an occasion of man lining his pockets with silver and gold. It was the absolute condemnation and commercialization of what man does to undo the sacred and the holiness of God.

God has you and I marked for greatness, but it can only come to fruition when we become transparent in our actions that shed light on the transforming work of God. The works of deception describe a false you, that paints you with limitations that God has not put on you. It is the laziness of not putting in the work that is instilled in you to have major success. Let us move forward in humility, whereby the heart and mind are working together to produce a prosperous and productive life for all.

Prayer: God, give me a clean heart and renew a right spirit within me. Make me an open vessel that can be used by You for Your glory. Make me as transparent as the city streets of pure gold that sit outside of those twelve pearly gates. Let my life be seen as one who desires to want more of You and not a passing shadow of myself. Use me for Your glory and the building of Your magnificent kingdom. Amen

God Demonstrates Grace

The word *grace* is so readily accepted but so easily overlooked. This was not so in the biblical days before the conception of Jesus and the shedding of His blood.

And surely your blood of your lives will I require; at the hand of every beast will I require it, and at the hand of man; at the hand of every man's brother will I require the life of man. (Genesis 9:5 KJV)

Many people of faith have pondered if the Bible spoke of two different Gods, for there seems to be a stark contrast in the behavior of God in the Old Testament and God in the New Testament. Church historians looked at this Scripture and struggled with seeing the God of love demanding the blood from one of His creatures. What puzzles us is that Jesus, the Son of God, who mirrors the work of His Father, is often seen showing compassion and healing those who needed help. The New Testament gives clear testimony of Jesus's willingness to help and to heal everyone who came to Him.

Near the end of the first century A..D. Gnosticism was on the move, and it gave great consternation to the Christian Church. Gnosticism was a movement that undermined the teaching of Jesus's Apostles, for they claimed to have more knowledge of God than those who were commissioned to preach the good news. One of their prominent leaders was a man named Marcion, who decided to create his own version of the Bible by illuminating any scripture that portrayed God as evil and mean. Marcion believed that the bible was misleading the people of God by painting this false narrative of Yahweh, who forced punishment on those who broke His law.

Looking at it through the lens of Marcion, we do read of some cases that make us scratch our heads. Take the story of Uzzah, who reached out to grab the ark of the covenant before it hit the ground and God smote him. (2 Samuel 6:3-7) It is a human reaction of someone grabbing something of importance before it can be broken. How about the narrative of a certain man in the woods on the Sabbath Day rubbing two sticks together to stay warm. Some witnesses saw him and took him to Moses and Aaron for judgment. Moses, in turn, prayed to God for guidance and God said that the man should be stoned to death for he broke the law. (Numbers 15:32-36) We must remember that behind every great attribute that God displays is His holiness. God must remain holy in everything that He does. The seraphims cry out that God is holy, holy, holy; the theological name *The Trisagion*, meaning three times holy. (Isaiah 6:3 KJV) The significance of this is that these angels are expressing the holiness of God in the superlative form.

Here is where the term grace becomes a welcoming ally to those who have fallen short of God's glory. As many would believe, grace did not just show up in the days of Jesus walking the streets of Galilee, but grace was demonstrated when Adam and Eve committed the first sin. God covered each of them with fig leaves so that their nakedness would not be seen. This is symbolic of God's love to show grace by shedding the blood of an animal to cover the sin that was before Him. God did not kill Adam nor Eve, but an animal to preserve their presence in society. So, today, we are the recipients of God's grace through the atoning act of Jesus Christ, who shed His blood for the remission of our sins.

Whom God hath set forth to be a propitiation through faith in His blood, to declare His righteousness for the remission of sins that are past, through the forbearance of God; (Roman 3:25 KJV)

The God of the Bible is the same God in the New Testament as in the Old Testament. He displays His grace from generation to generation. His mercy faileth not, and His loving-kindness is always on display.

Prayer: May we grow and learn of God's goodness and the grace that is afforded to us. May it have a sweet spot in our spirit that speaks of God's love and how He demonstrates it to people who have fallen short. Amen

Doing Life Together

One of the staples of the church that is consistently whispered in the ear of every member is that you are not to forsake the assembly of one another. In layman's terms, come to church. The idea is to create a mindset that parallels going to work in your vocation. You are expected to be present. This is man putting his fellow man on blast and ascribing to the notion that God would be angry if you were not present. But here is a good reason for each of us to be connected in fellowship: God's presence is felt in the midst of the believing saints. The word felt is the past participle of the word to feel, which refers to a sensation of something other than by sight.

A fitness coach would tell you that you would get a more efficient workout if you came to the gym with other like-minded people exercising. One reason is that your heart and mind are galvanized to accomplish that set goal when you see others beside you striving for that same mark. Oscillated from that community of people, your workout would suffer, and you would not be challenged. Likewise, striving to get stronger in your faith has its benefits when you are doing it together with other Believers. As a child of God, we are called to move from the act of receiving salvation to becoming mature in our spiritual walk.

Doing life together is a great way of exercising your gifts and gleaning from others who have a different spiritual calling than you. This connection helps bring support to those who may be deficient in that area where you are mature.

Nay, much more those members of the body, which seem to be more feeble, are necessary. (1 Corinthians 12:22 KJV)

The Bible Believers Commentary puts it this way: The kidneys, on the surface, seem not to be as strong as the arms, but the kidneys are indispensable whereas the arms are not. We can still have life if we lose an arm, but without the vital organ of the kidney, we can not survive. You can have a Bible in your hand, but if you can not understand the hermeneutics of scripture, you will not get the full import of what is being said. This is one reason why the Spirit of God has given the Church Believers who are equipped with various gifts to edify one another in those areas where help is needed. (1 Corinthians 12:4-25).

What is understood is that our giftedness is not something that we acquired on our own, but it was endowed in us through the divine insights of the Spirit of God. This means that God sowed this spiritual gift in you to be used to edify the body of believers in the area where their faith is weak. In the troubles of Job, after being further discouraged by his three miserable comforters, God sent Elihu to speak words of wisdom. Elihu premised his words by first saying that he drew his words from the deep truths of God.

For truly my words shall not be false: He that is perfect in knowledge is with thee. (Job 36:4 KJV)

This is what Job needed to hear that God's presence was with him. We can bear the pain when His touch is felt, for we know that our help is on the way. God has ordained you as His instrument of redemption to stand in the gap to lift those who are hurting. His Spirit has equipped and empowered you to be hands to draw out the absence and abandonment of feeling alone. God called Elihu because he was in the position to be used for the Lord's bidding.

Elihu also proceeded, and said, Suffer me a little, and I will show thee that I have yet to speak on God's behalf. (Job 36:1-2 KJV)

Elihu spoke positivity into the life of Job, bringing hope and a message of healing. Elihu was not off in the fields doing his own thing, but in fellowship with the Believers, using his gift for edification and the equipping of the saints. As a Believer, God has commissioned you for a major and majestic work that will manifest much fruit. It all starts with using your spiritual gifts to glorify the Lord.

Prayer: O Lord, my God, how excellent is it for Believers to dwell together in worship, in work, and the willingness to help one another. I pray that You will give us the heart and mind to interact and interface with each other as we travel this life's journey. Give us the spirit to bear one another's burdens and to be our brother's keeper. May our friendship be insulated with Christ's love and His peace. Amen

The Life Of The Party

What person does not like a great party? The thrill and the frills of mingling with friends and meeting new acquaintances is a momentous occasion to look forward to. Next, you have the venue and the decor that sets the atmosphere for an exciting and exhilarating experience. Finally, we have the appetizers, followed by the delectable main course that is washed down in the beverage of your choice.

What happens if one or more of these variables are missing and how does it affect the overall experience? A Jewish wedding is one of the most acclaimed and attended ceremonies that depicts the importance of having everything right. One of the pivotal elements that was necessary for the sustainability of the function was to have plenty of wine on tap. Wine is a spiritual component of many Jewish rituals, but it also has the physical capacity to add cheer to the hearts of men. It has its deep roots in symbolizing the joy of a man and a woman uniting in marriage. The Hebrew term *qiddush,* which comes over to the English as kiddush, means a blessing over the ceremony.

In John 2, there is a story of Jesus, His mother, and His disciples attending a wedding feast in Cana of Galilee. A major part of planning for a celebration is deciding on what guests you are going to invite. Some planners look to invite the leading socialites, while others seek out the high profile celebrities. But it is always a wise decision to woo a person like Jesus. What I am referring to is someone who has the resume of perfecting your party where it becomes the talk of the town.

The mother of Jesus was seasoned at planning for such occasions as a wedding. So, when the wine ran out, she led the master of the ceremony immediately to Jesus.

When the wine was gone, Jesus's mother said to Him, "They have no wine." (John 2:3 NIV)

Jesus was literally the life of the party; without the wine, the celebration would have stopped. The ceremonial and the spiritual application that was a major part of the Jewish ritual was coveted in the wine. The bridegroom had the job of making sure that there was a great supply of wine and to always have it available. It is like Jesus, so dependable, always available to hear our prayers and to answer our petitions. So, not only did Jesus save the wedding celebration, but He stepped into the role of the bridegroom, which was a foreshadowing of His marriage to the Church.

The mindset of Jesus's mother should mirror how we approach a problem: no matter how great or small, we take it to the Lord in prayer. The scripture is quick to point out that when Mary (Jesus's mother) realized that the wine was running out; she presented the problem to Jesus, for she had the faith to believe He had the power to fix it. What a spiritual lesson for us to glean. Placing our faith in Jesus trumps worrying about a problem that we have no power to resolve. Jesus tells the servants of the master of the ceremony to fill the water pots with water and then serve it to the guests. The book of James tells us that we must ask in faith without wavering to the commands of God. The servants were obedient to the voice of Jesus, and their problem was met with a prosperous ending.

But when you ask, you must believe and not doubt, because the one who doubts is like a wave of the sea, blown and tossed by the wind. (James 1:6 NIV)

When this new wine was presented at the wedding feast, the guests marveled that it tasted better than the wine that was set out first. This was quite remarkable, for most hosts set out the best wine first and afterward the inferior one. This is the faith that God wants us to have: He has the power to make your future years greater than your past.

Prayer: Jesus, You are the Lord of the Harvest. Everything created has its dependency on Your power to manifest change for the good. May we be living stones that wait patiently for You to move us from lacking to having an abundance. We trust and believe that You will continue to supply all our needs according to Your riches and glory. Amen

God allows U-turns

There is a universal negative that each one of us can draw from. We all have made some mistakes, and regret has come back to haunt us. The Scripture tells us that God sees everything, and nothing passes His desk unnoticed. But the grace of God is not like the unforgiving soul of man. He has an understanding heart that recognizes our fallen condition. That we all walk with the feet of clay, and our legs collapse at the sight of our errors.

Like as a father pitieth his children, so the LORD pitieth them that fear Him. For He knoweth our frame; He remembereth that we are dust. (Psalm 103:13-14 KJV)

How comforting it is to know that God, who is perfect in all His ways, grants second chances to those who have a cloudy background.

Zacchaeus was a man who had many riches but was bankrupt in his relationship with people. He was the chief publican in the town of Jericho. A publican was a Jew who was despised by other Jews, for they worked with the Roman government to collect taxes and levy high penalties on those who could not pay. They created their wealth by charging the people an exorbitant amount of money that exceeded what they were to collect. On a certain day, Jesus was passing through the town of Jericho, and Zacchaeus was close by. How many of us know that this was a divine assignment for Jesus, for everything that God does has a purpose, much like the Lord meeting the Samaritan woman at Jacob's well. (John 4:4-26) Zacchaeus got word that Jesus was coming his way, so he decided to position himself to see the Lord. There is something about shifting our eyes away from the affairs of the world and placing them on the Lord that breathes hope into our circumstances. Zaccheaus was a very short man and could not see over the crowd, so he climbed up a tree to see Jesus passing by. Reading these words would make you wonder what happened to change this man's demeanor to seek after the righteous God. Those who operate in the dark want to stay in the dark, for it hides their evil ways.

When the Spirit of God touches the soul of a person, no matter how degenerate they are, change is manifested. Jesus sees Zaccheaus and singles him out. This has the sensation of God leaving the 99 to find that one who is lost. This is the picture of every Believer: we were walking alone and lost on the street called destruction, until God singled us out and rescued us. Jesus tells Zaccheaus to come down from the tree, but the words of compassion and care echoed in the atmosphere. God was preparing Zaccheaus for a U-turn.

When Jesus reached the spot, He looked up and said to him, "Zaccheaus, come down immediately. I must stay at your house today." (Luke 19:5 NIV)

I love the New International Version, for it uses the word immediately. In Greek, the word *immediately* refers to having no time to elapse. God does not linger when His eyes are set on you for a new beginning. When the voice of God connects with the spirit man or spirit woman inside of you, your mindset shifts. After Zaccheaus heard the words of Jesus, his theology was changed, and he spoke with a contrite heart.

*And Zaccheaus stood, and said unto the Lord;
Behold, Lord, the half of my goods I give to the
poor; and if I have taken any thing from any
man by false accusation, I restore him fourfold.
(Luke 19:8 KJV)*

**Prayer: Lord, I come to You this day asking
that in this season of unfulfilled hopes and
dreams, You will grant us a U-turn so that we
may place our spiritual eyes on You. Let us
glean from the actions of Zacchaeus and position ourselves to walk upright with grace so
that we may eat with You at that great feast
with the Father.**

Our Firm Foundation

One thing that amazes me about the Bible is the parables that Jesus taught to the multitude and to His opponents. The message was empowering to those who had an open heart to receive God's word and a rebuke to those who rejected biblical truth. The parable found a home near the heart of those ears that were open to receive it, and it stiffened the neck of those whose eyes were closed to embrace it. The word parable comes from the Latin word *parabola,* which means a comparison. Likewise, the Greek word parable refers to the likeness or similitude. The use of parables in the bible was to bring to spiritual truths to some and to keep them hidden from others.

One of the most familiar parables that Jesus spoke was centered around the foundation that the word of God rested upon in the soul of a person. Jesus often used agricultural terminology when speaking to His audience, for their everyday experience involved the commerce of farming. Today, God speaks to us in a manner using the climate that surrounds our circumstances. In Luke 8:4-15, Jesus uses figurative language to express a kingdom principle. He speaks of the Sower, the seed, and the soil. The principle that Jesus wants His audience to remember is that every person is dealing with the same Sower and that we all get the same seed, but the soil is where the difference comes into play. During the pandemic, we all were facing the same problem and we all were given the same instructions on how to stay safe, but the condition of our immune system played a major role in who remained out of danger.

In any building project, the first thing that is checked is the foundation, for they need to know if it can support the expectations of the project. Jesus gives four types of foundations and the root cause of their collapse or culpability of standing. We must keep in mind that we are speaking of realistic results and how they relate to spiritual matters. The first is the wayside, which men trample over, and later, the birds devour it. This speaks of the care of God's word, how it is soaked up in the eardrum of the listener and then absorbed in the bloodstream for understanding. Jesus now speaks to those who hear God's word, and it falls on the rocky surfaces which lack the moisture to make the infrastructure smooth. The principle is that

God's word must nourish with His Spirit who deposits it in your heart, the understanding of the parable. Oftentimes, we have ears to hear, but our level of faith is small, and we fail to move forward because we are trusting in ourselves. The seed is planted, but we must remember that God does the watering in order for it to cultivate, or it will wither away. Jesus next takes up the foundation of God's word, being surrounded by thorns, which chokes out the growth to maintain the support that it has been given. When you hear a Rhema word that speaks of spiritual matters concerning your destiny, be aware that the thorns of life come to destroy that expectancy of a great harvest. The thorns can be the outside voices that come to rob you of your peace and joy. What an indictment to the testimony of God's truth for your life. The Apostle Paul said, when I would do good, evil is always around me. The adversary is always looking for ways to get you to forsake the promises of God. He is the father of lies and deception. Finally, Jesus gives His audience the good news that the person who is in a position to be blessed will have their heart prepared to receive God's word with readiness. This means that upon hearing the promises of God, they acquiesce in exact obedience to observe every-thing that the Lord says.

So, what is the significance of Jesus's parable? I believe He is speaking to the importance of guarding your heart so that the enemy cannot cause spiritual damage to what has been sown in your spirit. God has aligned great works to follow you in this season. He does not want it to be derailed by anything that will abort that seed that has been deposited in your spirit.

Above all else, guard your heart, for everything you do flows from it. (Proverbs 4:23 NIV)

In the ancient days, cities were guarded by walls, from the time of Hammurabi of Babylon to the Ming Dynasty. These walls were massive with great thickness and some held chariot races on the top for entertainment. The purpose of these walls was to protect and secure the people living in those cities. This is the picture of guarding your heart, putting up walls to insulate the sanctity of God's word that is being sown in you. What this parable is expressing to us is that the Sower, who is God, and the seed, which is the word, are both good. It was the soil that spoiled the outcome.

Prayer: God, we come to You with an open heart that is ready to hear and receive that precious word that is sent to nourish the soul and grow us up in our spirit. May it be a manifold blessing that will reap much in due season.

Seeing Through Spiritual Eyes

One of the essential tools that God gave to man is vision. It is the power of anticipating what is to come next. Along with the gift of vision, man was given the power to manifest change to a certain degree under God's sovereign rule. But with any tool, there come directions that will help you to operate it properly so that the effectiveness is exteriorized. Likewise, God gives mankind rules on how to use the eyes so that the greater good will benefit his life.

Do not be wise in your own eyes; fear the LORD and shun evil. (Proverbs 3:7 NIV)

Just as we confess that what we speak out of our mouth has the power to come to fruition, the eye is the entity that helps the body stay balanced and adjust to different conditions in life. Your eyes are the lamp to your body, and when you look for the goodness in life, it will find it. (Matthew 6:22) This was a metaphor that Jesus taught to the multitude concerning the difference between light and darkness. If the eye is full of light, then the uplifting and prosperous things of life will be manifested in it. But, if the eye focuses on evil, then darkness will flood the body. Jesus explained that the eye is the part of the body where spiritual illumination takes place, and the supernatural power of God can produce a greater faith in us. This means that we cannot walk around with closed minds and stiff necks to predetermine what God has ordained. Sometimes, God will put you in a cumbersome position where your circumstances are dire, and the only way out is through Him.

In 2 Kings 6:8-23, there is a story that speaks of God showing Himself strong to protect and to save the life of His servant. To set the story in the proper context, a little background information is needed. The king of Syria was planning a secret attack against the Israelites, but his plan was revealed and had to be revised. This happened not once but twice. So, the king of Syria sent out a search team to see who was the spy that was leaking this secret information. The report came back and it was told that the man of God, Elisha, was giving the king of Israel the inside information. Elisha was now a person of interest and had a bull's eye on his back.

On a certain morning, the servant of Elisha went out and discovered that they were surrounded by horses, chariots, and a great host of the Syrian army. The servant quickly told this to the man of God with tremendous fear, expecting that this was their fatal end. We are told repeatedly in the scriptures to fear not, for the ALMIGHTY God is with us. That He is our refuge and strength, a very present help in the time of trouble. Even if the waters roar and be troubled and the mountains be shaken, God is in the midst of the situation. The Bible declares that we have a powerful weapon in our toolbelt, that is, prayer.

And Elisha prayed, and said, LORD, I pray thee, open his eyes, that he may see. And the LORD opened the eyes of the young man; and he saw: and, behold, the mountain was full of horses and chariots of fire round about Elisa. (2 Kings 6:17 KJV)

Using your weapon of prayer can war off the enemy's attack against you. In the case of Elisa and his servant, God used a protective host to camp around them for protection. What the servant saw with his physical eyes was not the same vision that Elisa saw with his spiritual eyes. Your eyes are to line up with the Giver of it and how He manifests His power in it.

Prayer: Heavenly Father, I come to You seeking the diligence and the dependency on You. May we lean more on our spiritual eyes so that our second glance will give us a true picture of reality. As we move by faith, may we be encouraged by Your Spirit that surrounds us and insulates us with protection to proceed on the pathway that You have set for us. May You find a finished work in us that will make our joy full. Amen

More Than I Can Bear

May you never experience the season of having the difficulties of life heap up and put a stranglehold on your faith. It is an arduous and uncomfortable feeling to reach out for hope and find it amiss. In those dark and dismal moments that is when your faith in God should be at its strongest point. There is no test or trial that He does not have the power to resurrect from and to restore you to. We must remember that God is not oblivious to our cares and concerns. He orchestrates all things under His command to do His bidding. Even the devil knows that nothing happens unless God gives it the power to be so. The picture is that we are never to lose hope in the staying power of God to resurrect us from our grime situation. It just might be that God is working behind the scenes to strengthen our faith and fortify His word in our spirit.

In Genesis 42:29-38, we get a story whereby God pulls back the curtains so that we can see the candidates He uses to bring His glory to His name. I know that you might be saying, is there a special type of person that God seeks to bless? Is there a criteria that must be met in order to be considered? Yes, God searches for the one that seeks after Him.

The LORD looked down from heaven upon the children of men, to see if there were any that did understand, and seek God. (Psalms 14:2 KJV)

In this day, there was a famine throughout the world, and the only place that had food was Egypt. Jacob, the patriarch of the nation of Israel, sent his ten sons to Egypt to get grain so that the family and their cattle would survive. At this moment in time, Jacob had already believed that he had lost one son to death at the hands of some vicious animals, so he was vigilant in protecting the remaining sons from any more tragedies. While Jacob's ten sons were in Egypt to get the necessary food items, they were accused of being spies, and to prove their inno-cence, they were forced to leave one of the brothers behind.

The brothers went back to Canaan to face their father and told him the whole story. To give you some added content, the youngest son, Benjamin, was now being used as a bargaining chip to get more grain and the release of the brother left in Egypt. Benjamin was the son of Jacob's old age and the one that he kept close to. The name Benjamin in Hebrew means the son of my right hand. Have you ever had someone so dear to you that you kept them close and clung to their whereabouts? They were the apple of your eye, and now came the moment for you to let them go. Can you feel the anxiety and the anguish that is brewing inside of Jacob? As the days of the famine increased, Jacob's hope of keeping everyone safe was falling apart at the seams. The plot began to thicken when the brothers opened their bags and found that the money to purchase the grain was not removed. This became a major crisis in the eyes of Jacob and his fear began to multiply. Finally, the grain ran out and it was time for the brothers to take another trip to Egypt. The pressure was mounting up on Jacob; although he was a man of faith, his heart was failing inside of him. We speak of faith as if it is something that can be taught and mastered in one online class. I am sure that Job would say otherwise. We can be put to the test whereby all we see and feel is the walls closing in on us, but the scripture is clear that God never puts more on our plate than what we can handle. In those difficult times, the presence of God draws nigh unto us for strength and the steadfastness to endure.

Jacob now had lost two sons, and the third was in danger, for he was the bargaining chip for the exchange for food and the release of his older brother. In moments of stress and solaceness, a person can feel the impact of solitude despite being surrounded by comforters. Jacob, forced by the severity of the famine, sends Benjamin with his brothers to retain more grain. He puts double the amount of money in the backpack of each of his sons for the first supply of grain, which was not paid for. Jacob's sons are now en route to face the man who gave them much consternation and dread. It is said that the longest and the loneliest walk is when you are about to face the unknown. If the story would end here, it would be absent from God's gospel, which is His good news.

If we would take the time to reflect on God's providence, we would see that His fingerprints are smeared all over our destiny to defeat the enemy who comes against us. What Jacob did not know was that the Lord was working everything out for his good and his household. God's plan is twofold: it secures a happy ending for you, but it also reaffirms His divine plan to redeem. Jacob's hope of keeping his family together was established. Every one of his beloved sons lived and they became the foundation of the Israel nation.

Prayer: O gracious God, my hands are lifted high to give praise and adoration to You. It is by Your right hand that we are not consumed by the problems and difficulties that life presents. I take great comfort that You are my refuge, a high tower that I can run to for safety. You are my buckler and my shield, destroying the enemies that have launched an attack against me. Thank you for covering and comforting me in the season when troubles rise above what I can handle. May my faith continue to rest in You alone. Amen

Be A Mighty Thoroughbred

The thoroughbred horse is one of the most graceful and glorified mammals in God's kingdom. From his chiseled head to his muscle-carved chest, this mammal is elegantly built for agility and speed. The thoroughbred is known for his temperament and being high-spirited, which attests to his diligence and his extraordinary work ethic. These are much-needed qualities that we as human beings need to garner in order to weather life's storms in an efficient way. When trials and tribulations are staring you in the face, the inclination to remain calm is a difficult task to do. The rationale is to get upset and complain because the optimism of hope has been invaded. It is said that we all should be prisoners of hope, for, without it, our aspirations for survival are diminished. This is what God wanted His prophet Jeremiah to recognize. That He was the hope of Israel for a better tomorrow. The gospel artist Emeli Sande sings in her song, Breathing Underwater, "If we can hold on to all the love that we borrowed, then today will be jealous of tomorrow." You and I need to stand firm and place our faith not in what makes a guest appearance today, but in the reality that tomorrow brings.

If you have raced with men on foot and they have worn you out, how can you compete with horses? (Jeremiah 12:5a NIV)

After Jeremiah addressed God over the idea of the wicked prospering and the righteous having a tough road to travel, God told him that he would see more bitter concerns ahead. This is a message to each of us when we see the disadvantaged and the destitute not getting their fair portion. We struggle with the consternation of some receiving the blessings from God's hand and others seem to be forgotten. It is like rolling up your sleeves to help with a quick fix, but turning a blind to a natural disaster that is out of your hands. There is pain associated in both cases: one has temporal implications to need and the other can leave a permanent mark of death.

Let's get a little more personal. Suppose you are wrestling with trying something new in your craft and the pressure to compete is constantly weighing on you. It is in your heart to master these amazing gifts that God has placed in you, but the struggle comes in taking those first steps. I know it has been said that the initial steps are the hardest, but it has been proven that the staying power to compete is fierce and foreboding. So, what do you do when you find it hard to keep up with the footman, not to think about the opportunity of running with the horses in your field? You have a Jeremiah moment by holding on to God's promises and His provisions to see you through to the finish line. This is God's signature move. He always keeps His promise and walks with us until it is complete.

Insomuch that we desired Titus, that as he had begun, so he would also finish in you the same grace also. (2 Corinthians 8:6 KJV)

Titus had a great idea of collecting money to help the people in Jerusalem who were trying to get back on their feet after a severe famine. Titus went to Corinth, the wealthiest church in modern-day Greece, to put this plan into motion, but the people were not willing. If Titus was like me, this project would have failed, for I struggle to no end when I hear the words of rejection. One thing that we can count on is that God always has a remnant to do His will. So, Titus got some encouragement from the poorest church, which was in Macedonia, who gave freely. I can hear the voice of God whispering in the ear of Titus and us today:

Being confident of this, that he who began a good work in you will carry it on to completion until the day of Christ Jesus, (Philippians 1:6 NIV)

When you find the road ahead is more demanding and the task ahead is daunting, lean on the Sovereign Lord who will infuse in you the strength of the thoroughbred and his steadfastness to endure to the end.

Prayer: Heavenly Father, I ask that You put a fire in the belly of Your people that will not be distinguished during difficult times. Make them strong-willed, walking on hind feet, ready to scale any wall to see what the end that You have for them. Amen

Are You A Cheerleader

I am asking this question in the critical sense, for the world needs more people who discern the gift of compassion. When we speak words of edification and empowerment into a person's life, it gives them the inner strength to stand still and not give up. Telling that person you are in their corner gives them the fortitude to remain faithful and to fight on. When we share our testimony, it gives validity to the message so that hope remains the centerpiece as they move forward.

Therefore encourage one another and build each other up, just as in fact you are doing. (1 Thessalonians 5:11)

A co-worker gets good news of a promotion, and it generates a better quality of life for him and his family. Do you root for them in their elevation, or do you murmur because it is not your blessing? When you hear a conversation of concern that a loved one is sick, do you say a prayer for their healing or find reasons for their sickness? The Apostle Paul says the more excellent way is to rejoice with them that do rejoice and weep with them that are weeping. (Romans 12:15) The word *"parakaleo"* comes from the Greek to mean one who is called to come alongside. It is the position that mirrors the Spirit of God, who is the Believer's paraclete.

The Apostle Paul starts off chapter 12 by exhorting the people of God to have a transformed mind and to not follow what the world dictates. He says that we are to be transformed by the renewing of our minds, which illustrates the perfect will of God. The world has the tendency to show a covetous spirit when someone gets elevated to a greater status. If we adopt this mindset that their joy should be mine, this becomes a direct rebuke to God and His authority to hand out blessings. We must remember that God has a purpose and a plan that satisfies His glory, not the exalting of a man. When we embrace this oracle, it will help us in our consecration as Christians to mirror the attributes of Christ Jesus.

When the Lord walked the earth, He demonstrated the gift of compassion to the sick, the hurting, the lost, and the forgotten. He ministered to their souls and poured into them, demonstrating the intimate relationship that God wants with His children.

One of the characteristics of being a cheerleader is to not think too highly of yourself but to be sober-minded and to remember that it is not about you. You are positioned to equip and encourage them, displaying patience so that this moment is nourished in love. This is what the Apostle calls your conduct in humility, as a vessel for the Almighty God.

The Scripture says that we are to love without dissimulation. Showing the affection that advocates a spirit of hospitality. Meaning that we are not to mask our love towards them in their experience. We are to be cheerleaders, being vocal, having their back, not throwing shade or giving a smokescreen that could cause an invisible scar on their heart.

Suppose we could go back and reflect on the first homicide recorded in Scripture. In that case, we will see that the principle of celebrating one's achievements had not yet settled in the spirit of mankind.

And Cain talked with Abel his brother: and it came to pass, when they were in the field, that

Cain rose up against Abel his brother, and slew him. (Genesis 4:8 KJV)

Both Abel and Cain gave sacrifices to God from the fruit of their labor. Abel was a keeper of sheep, and he gave the first of his flock to God. Likewise, Cain was a tiller of the ground, and he gave the first of his fruit from the ground. The sacrifice of Abel was accepted, and the one from Cain was rejected. In the sovereign nature of God, Cain understood the posture of the sacrifices and how it was to be given. The indication is that Abel gave his sacrifice as a sacrificial gift pleasing to God, while Cain displayed a grudging spirit that displeased God. (Genesis 4:6-7) So Cain rose up and killed Abel instead of commending his brother and seeing what he did that was good in God's eyes. When we lack the familiarity of displaying affection to one another, it opens the door for hatred to come in.

Prayer: Lord, I ask that You would raise up an army of cheerleaders that will be in a position to strengthen those who are struggling with insecurities and doubts. Make them instruments for Your glory. Amen

Manipulating The Masses

One of the character traits that man has possessed since infancy days of him walking the earth, is the act of manipulation to get the upper hand through skillful influence. Man has a hunger to feed his earthly desires, so that he can manage the situation to maneuver a change that will fit his purpose. In the final analysis, it is about control and making himself completely comfortable. The Etymology of manipulation comes from the method of digging an ore, which is a metal-bearing mineral close to the sulfur family. It had its genesis in the eighteenth century as the method of handling people. There is a major difference between handling a piece of metal and manipulating a precious living soul. God gave man the right to have dominion over creation, not another man.

In John 9:13-41, there is a story that depicts the powers to be that slay over the frail and the weak. It is a man using his position and power to manipulate the masses from exercising their right of freedom to worship. Jesus performed a miracle restoring sight to a blind man, which is a good and a great thing. The problem was that it was done on the Sabbath Day. The crowd that witnessed this awesome move of God must have thought that spreading this news would generate a buzz that would bolster the faith of Israel. But instead, it aroused the religious leaders, who were afraid of losing their place as the keepers of the synagogue. You would think that the religious leaders would have been excited for the blind man and eager to announce to the world that the God of Israel is the only God that can perform miracles. Shockingly, what took place was not the news of the blind man given sight to see, but judging Jesus as either a righteous man or a sinner.

How man continues to miss the move of God and His visitation to restore what is broken. If the religious leaders had allowed their hearts to be nourished in God's word, they would have recognized that the sabbath was never meant to prevent acts of mercy or kindness. The law was always to come under the umbrella of love. In this case, it is miraculously giving a man the opportunity to see like other human beings. Manipulation can lead to misguided leaders trying to interfere on what God is trying to do, in this case, the power of a miracle.

But the Jews did not believe concerning him, that he had been blind, and received his sight, until they called the parents of him that had received his sight. (John 9:18 KJV)

The etymology of the word *miracle* comes from the Latin to mean an act that causes wonder and astonishment. So, in layman's terms, this refers to an inexplicable act by normal standards. The religious leaders were accustomed to seeing miracles whenever God sent His vessel to speak on His behalf. So, their reluctance to receive this miracle performed by Jesus was an act of controlling the masses to not accrue worship to the Son of God.

The religious leaders made a pronouncement that anyone caught giving Jesus praise would be cast out of the synagogue and forbidden to participate in the worship exercises. (John 9:19-22) Manipulation to control the mind is the evilest act committed to another human being.

Today, we have many Christians who live in fear and are persecuted for their faith in Jesus Christ. Their suffering is not just being put out of the synagogues, but they are paying for it with their very life. The cry out for help is massive and many are stepping up to show support for these victims.

Prayer: Lord, I come to You with a spirit of compassion to come alongside those who are suffering from physical, mental and spiritual abuse. Let those who are strong stand in the gap to bear the burdens of those who are hurting. May we be a voice that cries out in the wilderness for those who are persecuted for their faith in You. Paul admonishes us to do nothing in vainglory but esteem others above ourselves. Heavenly Father, I ask that You give

us the mind of Christ Jesus, who is the defender of those who can not defend themselves. Amen

The Instruction And The Application

Whenever we are introduced to a new product or service, a rule of thumb is to read the instructions before we begin to move into the operation of it. This is key, for often, there are small steps that are essential in making sure the product or service works efficiently. More importantly, these steps are integrated into the function of making sure of its durability and safety while it is in operation. One of the benchmarks of distinguishing the writings of Paul to his apostolic counterparts was found in his giving of instructions and the application to the churches. He would give information concerning the subject matter and then would dedicate the second half of the letter to the application to show its effectiveness. The apostle believed giving equal weight to the instruction and its application would show the importance of not only your results, but how you got there.

In Exodus 14:14, Moses, the mediator of the Old Testament, was given charge by God to lead His people into the land of promise. Before taking strides toward that promise, the people were subdued and suffered cruel punishment from the hands of Pharaoh and the Egyptian people. The hardness of the Pharaoh's heart made it unbearable for the Israelites to survive. So, Moses, guided by the Spirit of God, spoke words of comfort to the Israelite people.

Do not be afraid. Stand firm and you will see the deliverance the LORD will bring you today. The Egyptians you see today you will never see again. (Exodus 14:13 NIV)

Here, we get an example of God's people getting instructions from Moses on how to have freedom and to be liberated from their oppressors. The first thing was for the people to have faith and believe the message from God's spokesperson. Moses said you must not be afraid. Have you ever encountered a situation that terrified you to no end? The characteristics of fear were embedded in the core of your being and, to have solace and peace, would be difficult. This was the Israelites' predicament. In the moments of an impasse, hearing from God is always the best advice. Moses told the people to stand still and wait for the deliverance from the

LORD. Here we have God's commander and chief barking out the instructions that will lead the application of deliverance.

The result is usually what we focus on, giving less consideration to the steps to make it happen. But I would say to you without the faith to follow the instructions, your application would have a different ending. Having the faith to trust in God and His word is the bridge to help you cross over to safety and to the peaceful shores of life. Many of us have experienced miracles of healing and dynamic outcomes from tumultuous situations because we heard the voice of God. The Israelites experienced their deliverance and they never saw their adversary again.

That day the LORD saved Israel from the hands of the Egyptians, and Israel saw the Egyptians lying dead on the shore. (Exodus 14:30 NIV)

Prayer: Heavenly Father, I thank You for showing us that following Your instructions and applying Your word will produce a greater outcome. I ask that You would help us to remember the immeasurable and immense importance of having faith in You to fight our battles no matter how difficult. May our eyes be open to witness You showing Yourself strong on our behalf, in Jesus' name.

Getting The Balance Right

In my college years, there was a lot of transition from being dependent and relying on my parents to becoming independent and self-reliant. My focus on the future and my finances took precedence, followed by clothes and the music that filled my ears, which shaped my worldview. In my college years, I became a big fan of Classic 80's Rock. The sound was incredible, a little pop with some catchy lyrics. At that time, my ears had an affinity with the group called Depeche Mode. This group rocked with songs such as: *"Everything Counts, "People Are People," "Strange Love" and "Personal Jesus."* One of their big hits that I often listened to was a song called *"Get The Balance Right."*

Be responsible, respectable

Stable but gullible

Concerned and caring

Help the helpless

But always remain

Ultimately selfish

Get the balance right Get the balance right

"Get the balance right" conveyed the message of having that happy medium, not in giving everything away whereby you become penniless, but overindulging in moderation, being a good steward of what you have. The weight of helping the poor and the needy is not placed on your narrow shoulders to carry. Jesus said you will always have the poor amongst you, but Me not always. (Matthew 26:11) The most important thing in life is to have a personal relationship with the God of the universe.

The opportunity to lend to the needy will always present itself, so the stewardship of it is the essence of how you should give. Getting the right balance will position your heart to be the motivating factor in your giving. Jesus uses a narrative that addresses the value of time versus money, so that we can be better stewards of what we have. There was a woman who had an alabaster box of a very precious ointment whose value exceeded 50 thousand dollars, according to some biblical scholars. The spiritual takeaway is that this woman was giving the greatest gift she had to Jesus. In an intimate relationship, you hold back nothing to show and demonstrate your love. Paul writes that God demonstrated His love towards us by dying on the cross to atone for our sins. (Romans 5:8) The balance is that both parties poured out acts of affection to show their love. Now, I am not saying that the value is the same. We can never match the loving-kindness of God, but the praise and worship that we give to His Son does not go unnoticed. This woman poured the entire bottle of expensive ointment on Jesus as an act of affection. We later read that it was used to anoint His body for His burial.

"Truly I tell you, wherever this gospel is preached throughout the world, what she has done will also be told, in memory of her" *(Matthew 26:13 NIV)*

At first glance, our giving may seem to be trivial to the person on the receiving end, but we must remember that we just sow and let God do the watering. The small seed that we have sown may reap a tremendous harvest in that person's life. That small seed that was sown on the fertile ground may have unlimited growing potential. The mindset of pettiness provides ammunition for the adversary to hold down the left out and the forgotten. We must not entertain the thoughts of those who need to be labeled as perfidy, ones who deliberately breach our trust to get a hand-out. Oftentimes, there is an underlying reason for the help and it might not have manifested itself in the present moment.

The importance of staying focused on your purpose is tied to your happiness and the fulfill-ment of your life. When God berth you into this world, He breathes into you a divine work that would precede any desire that would arbitrarily enter the domain of your thoughts. There were many times when Jesus healed or cast out a demon, He would tell them to not tell anyone about the miracle. One reason was that Jesus was more interested in fulfilling His mission from His Father. Remember, Jesus was born to bring the good news. A message of hope to those who were living in darkness and the promise of God's salvation to those who believed. Yes, Jesus wanted to heal every single person, but that was not His calling. His obedi-ence to the Father was a greater responsibility, which would benefit a myriad of people even unto the 21st century. Getting the right balance, means you need to hear the voice of God and take heed to His plan for your life.

Prayer: May the Lord God give you a heart of flesh that will yield to those who are in need. May your spiritual eyes see the hand of God using your gift to resurrect hope and compassion in that person's life. May it bear much fruit and yield a harvest of one hundredfold. Amen

The Promises of God are Yes and Amen

The trials and the tests in life can be overwhelming and can lead you to believe that there is no power on earth that can help you break the chains of defeat. The pressure that weighs on the spirit and the heaviness that lingers in the soul can make you forget about the promises that were given to you in that season. We recognize that when a person gives you their word, it is usually given in good faith. That is, they will make a genuine effort to get it done. But there are moments in history when your word takes a backseat to life's circumstances. In 1 Kings 18, God tells the Prophet Elisa to give word to the king of Israel concerning a great downpour of rain. I know that you may be thinking rain is not often associated with good news, but in this season in Israel, there was a severe famine.

Just a footnote, this was not the great famine that was recorded in the history books that lasted for seven years. (2 Kings 8:1) But anytime there is a famine, it creates a hardship for the people, the livestock and the land. The necessity of water is vital to your health, because it keeps your body temperature normal, while it lubricates your joints and protects the tissues in your body. It gives maintenance to the sustainability of the things that surround you. So, when Elisha spoke this promise to the king that the rain was coming, it was a time for rejoicing to all in Israel. After three and a half years, Elisa tells the king to get prepared for the rain that is about to come. But as human beings, we lack faith when there is a protracted amount of time between the promise and the fulfillment of it. In verse 41, Elisa goes to the king and encourages him to drink and take some nourishment to remain strong for the impending rain. This speaks to the character of Elisa, who trusts God with all his heart, no matter what the circumstances look like. This should be the posture of every Christian who places their faith in the Almighty God. His timing is always impeccable and immeasurable. His blessings meet our needs at the perfect time for the greatest results.

In verse 43, Elisa sent his servant to go towards the sea to see if the sign of rain was coming. The servant of Elisa came back with a message of false hope, but the persistence of the prophet prodded him to look again seven times. How many of us would have been discouraged after the first reply of not seeing the promise fulfilled? Here is where Elisa succeeded, and many of us have failed. The scripture records that Abraham, the father of our faith, waited patiently before seeing the promises of God.

And so, after he had patiently endured, he obtained the promise. (Hebrews 6:15 KJV)

Patience is key in obtaining the promises of God. God has never broken a promise that He has made. His promises are yes and amen. On the seventh try, the servant of Elisa saw a small cloud about the size of a man's hand. This is what Elisa needed a proof that God keeps His promises.

Prayer: Lord, I ask that you increase our faith so that doubt is not entertained in our hearts. May the remembrance of Your past testimonies be fresh in our minds. Help us to remain steadfast and unmovable in trusting You. Lord, we know that You have all the power to restore and to make anew everything that is broken. So, we will wait on Your perfect timing and the fulfillment of Your promises. Amen

Volatile Actions After A Victory

The thrill of victory and the agony of defeat ties our emotions in more than one way. There is a hormone in the human body called dopamine that is released in the nervous system when we get excited. This hormone acts in conjunction with the brain to regulate our emotions. So, when we experience a victorious moment, dopamine gives us a feeling of confidence; while facing defeat, it gives us a declaration of doubt in our abilities. The Apostle Paul suggests that we need to be careful in both cases, for the steps of evil are crouching at our door.

I find then a law, that, when I would do good, evil is present with me. (Romans 7:21 KJV)

Paul is saying that there is a principle here that we need to pay close attention to, that is: our good intentions have a way of leading us into a bad situation. We hear the slogan, win at any cost. What does this mean for our opponent and how do they react to this devastation?

In 1 Kings 19:1, we read the story of Elijah, who had just won a great victory for the LORD. Elijah set the record straight that the God of Abraham is the only true God that has the power over a famine and every circumstance that touches this earth. He had just defeated the 450 prophets of Baal, who declared that the god they served was greater and more powerful than the God of the scriptures. Baal was the Canaanite god of life and fertility and, it was also believed, that he had the power over the wind and the rain. So, if this was accurate, this was definitely the time for him to show up and show out, for the people were suffering in this famine.

Midday passed, and they continued their frantic prophesying until the time for the evening sacrifice. But there was no response, no one answered, no one paid attention. (1 Kings 18:29 NIV)

The people waited in great anticipation for the power of Baal to send down rain, but like any false deity, it can't do what only the LORD can do. After waiting patiently, there was no sign from Baal; therefore, Elijah called on the God of the Scripture to show Himself strong to end the famine. Elijah, like many of us, has seen God win many victories in the face of our enemies, which testifies that He is the only one worthy of our worship. In this moment, we have to reflect on Paul's words that remind us evil is close by after a victory. Elijah gets word that his life is now being threatened by the king's wife. Jezebel, who married the king out of a business arrangement, brought the worship of Baal to the house of Israel, along with the prophets whom Elijah just defeated. So, Elijah finds himself running for his life on the heels of winning a great victory for God.

Elijah was afraid and ran for his life. When he came to Beersheba in Judah, he left his servant there, while he himself went a day's journey. (I Kings 19:3-4a NIV)

The sounds of victory are wonderful, but we need to be just as sharp to endure the post-trauma that could be heading our way. Elijah ran from the point of his victory in Jezreel south-ward to Beersheba, which is about one hundred miles. In desperate times, the distance traveled is immeasurable to create a safe haven to harness our peace. What escaped the mind of

Elijah is that the God who gave him the victory over the prophets of Baal is the same God who could save his life. I like what David said after he had won many victories for the people of God. What profit is there in my blood when I go down to the pit? Shall the dust praise thee? Shall it declare thy truth? (Psalm 30:9 KJV) David was making the appeal to God that if his life was no more, how could glory come from it?! We need to have this forethought, for our Father in Heaven inhabits the praise from His children.

Prayer: Our Great God, how awesome is Your power to deliver us and sustain us from the grips of evil. May Your right hand be by our side for the provision to have success and the protection to cover us in the midst thereof. Amen

Send Me A Higher Love

What would you say is the foundation that stabilizes and gives you the support to function in society? Many would say that love is the essential element that knits it together for success. If we check the landscape, look at the division and the diversity of mankind, we could draw the conclusion that the natural nutrition of life requires the presence of God. Man does not have the fortitude to face the difficulties of life separated from God's power. Our sustainability is rooted in God's affectual love for His creation. His love defines nihilism, the power to manifest a way out when it seems that all hope is lost. So, there is a shift that is needed to change the mind of man to think that he is built to walk alone.

The artist Steven Winwood wrote a song called *Send Me A Higher Love.* Winwood addressed the darker side of not finding that love that can build an ark when there is a triennial downpour.

Things look so bad everywhere in this whole world. What is fair? We walk blind and we try to see falling behind in what could be.

Bring me a higher love. Bring me a higher love. Bring me a higher love. Where's that higher love I keep thinking of?

Mr. Winwood just needed to meditate on the words of Paul, coming from the book of Romans, the 8th chapter, where the apostle gives an apologetic response to the agape love of God. He says, "What can we say to these things? If God be for us, who can be against us?" (Romans 8:31) The rhetorical answer would be: as long as God is with you, your enemies would have no power over you. It is Christ Jesus who died for you and rose again, having all power to justify you to the Father. Paul closes his argument with this profound statement.

Who can separate us from the love of Christ? Shall tribulation, or distress, or persecution, or famine, or nakedness, or peril, or sword? (Romans 8:35 KJV)

The inspiration of the Holy Spirit put in the heart of Paul to cover every diverse thing that could separate the love of us from Christ Jesus. This speaks to the immutable love of Jesus, who cares for us like a shepherd for his sheep. There is not a moment that transitions in time that His eye is not on you and that His pastoral covering is not near you. David said that the Lord was always in front of him and guiding him.

"I saw the Lord always before me. Because He is at my right hand, I will not be shaken. (Acts 2:25 NIV)

David was giving confirmation that when divisive and destructive situations come into your life, the Lord is by your side for assurance and assistance to see you through. It is in that relationship we become conquerors who triumph over those challenges that try to impede our walk for a victorious life.

Prayer: Most gracious God, we thank you for drawing nigh unto us and granting us access to Your holy presence. We receive that higher love that surpasses any love that any man or woman can give us. May we never forget that nothing can separate us from your love. Amen

A Letter To The Reader

There are some things that you cannot put a price tag on, for the value is so incredible that it would scare off the casual observers. God's love for His creation fits in that category. Throughout the Scripture, we find that God is a pourer. He is constantly adding to our lives and growing us up in the maturation of His word. In spite of our grit and tenacity, we are still dependent on His tender care for us.

"Believing God" addresses some of the areas that we, as Believers, struggle with. We find ourselves reaching back to the world for answers that can only be gleaned from God. He uses the Person of Jesus, who is the living word, to equip and empower us with godly precepts that produce godly results.

I pray that you find this devotional practical and profitable as you grow in the knowledge and the faith that will keep your feet standing on fertile ground. It is His word that worketh in you to do His will so that you may enjoy the good pleasure of it.

Bibliography

1. Benitez-Eves, T., & Benitez-Eves, T.(2023b, July 13). The more Divine meaning behind "Higher Love" by Steve Winwood. *AmericanSongwriter*. https://american songwriter.com/the-more-divine-meaning-behind-higher-love-by-steve-winwood/

2. *Emeli Sandé - Breathing Underwater Lyrics Lyrics.com*(n.d.-b). https://www.lyrics.com/lyric/33352629/Breathing+Underwater

3. Britannica, The Editors of Encyclopaedia. "King James Version". Encyclopedia Britannica, 14 Aug. 2023, https://www.britannica.com/topic/King-James-Version. Accessed 28 August 2023.

4. *New International Version.* (2011). BibleGateway.com. http://www.biblegateway.com/versions/New-International-Version-NIV-Bible/#booklist

5. *American Standard Version (ASV) - Version Information - BibleGateway.com.*(n.d.). https://www.biblegate way.com/versions/American-Standard-Version-ASV-Bible/

6. *New Strong's Dictionary of Hebrew and GreekWords.* (1996). https://www.logos.com/product/1212/new-strongs-dictionary-of-hebrew-and-greek-words?

7. Thomas Nelson. (2021b, July 26). *Book Details ThomasNelson.*https://www.thomasnelson.com/9780840719720/believers-bible-commentary/

8. *Martin Luther | Encyclopedia.com.* (n.d.-b). https://www.encyclopedia.com/people/philosophy-and-religion/protestant-christianity-biographies/martin-luther

9. *Aristotlequotes*.(n.d.).https://quotefancy.com/aristotle-quotes

10. Lohnes, Kate. "Brave New World". Encyclopedia Britannica, 9 Nov. 2022, https://www.britannica.com/topic/Brave-New-World. Accessed 28 August 2023.

11. BroadStreetPublishing®,LLC. (2017b, October27). *Books-BroadStreet Publishing®*. BroadStreetPublishing®. https://broadstreetpublishing.com/prayers-and-promises-for-men/9781424564651/